TWO SPIRIT

TWO SPIRIT

STORIES, SEX, AND THE CEREMONY BEHIND
IT ALL

ALYCIA TWO BEARS

Print Book ISBN: 978-1-7388587-1-2

Editor: A. D. Boyd

Cover Artist: Serena Taylor

Author Photo Credit: Studio Lumen

THE JOURNEY

THE FOURTH ROUND
Send the ancestors home

THE FIRST ROUND

WELCOMING KIN AND ANCESTORS

Two Spirit Odes and Identity

whyte supremacy, access denied.

the shape of my brown eyes
the way my hair
holds in the heat of
the sun
my cheekbones
sloped and cut
like the mountains
I seek peace
from the fact
I come from this Land
my birth
a direct
refusal
in an ongoing
genocide
my whole existence is
political

Uncensored

"and who do you write for?"

                                    myself

                    to give love and affection
                        in the ways in which
                    I desire to be consumed
                        I will write myself
                            into a dizzy
                        warm my own skin
                        make myself drunk
            on words that lust after my thoughts

Texture Upon Texture

Elysian
Words have texture.
River rock smooth, running off the tongue.
Indian Act abrupt, forced to swallow.
People are like words.
Some are peanut butter peculiar.
Stuck to the top of my mouth, sucking my tongue.
Soul stokers. Euphoric. Ecstasy.
Everybody has their own consistency.
Pattern.
Composition.
Feel.

Mama Two Shoes had No Shoes

The first dream of the late Sharron Proulx-Turner.

We met on the mountainside. Soft, green moss is everywhere, with scattered pieces of grey stone. It isn't rocky, full of jagged edges or slippery shale fragments. The slope is steep, and I am afraid of slipping off the edge into oblivion. But not you. You tipsy toe around the moss and open spaces. Light. Delicate. You move with the strength and grace of a dancer. I watch your cherry-red flannel dress, with its small yellow and white flower print, flap in the wind while I rest cross-legged, holding tobacco and ribbon in my hand. I glance at my lap. My plain sunshine-yellow sweat dress also ripples with the breeze. When I look in your direction, my hair whips in the wind, blocking my view. I can't keep my sight on you to watch, observe, and learn from you. Your hair is long again. Really long. Past your waist. Before cancer, it was thick, shiny and white. Oh, how I miss that hair. My heart aches at the thought. And that's when I see our hair intertwine, dancing together in the wind—a mix of brown and white. This breeze is strong, yes, but holds no chill. It simply swirls around us. When I first hear them, I scan the landscape. Then I see them running. Laughing. Full of joy. Free. My children. My blessings. One would think they were born of the mountain we are perched on, with no fear of falling. I call out to them to be careful around the edge. My voice is caught in the wind and carries away from their sweet ears. My daughter turns and smiles at me. With a slight turn of the head again, you smile at them, look back at me and mouths, "They're gonna be alright, Mama, let them be." I believe you. I always have. I stand with your encouragement. Despite the fear of being blown over the cliff, I rise, clutching the tobacco in my palm. I raise the tobacco offering, standing tall and proud. I wonder, why this mountain? Why this place? This day? I follow your gaze. It's fixed on the valley below. Small, green, beautiful in its lush scenery. I hear another voice from just beside me, an unknown woman. She says, "That's her home y'know. That valley. She just needed to see it. This is the only place she can see it from." We let our tobacco go, spreading it wherever it needs to be received. Letting our prayers spill all over the mountain.

Barb

steam rolls off the top
of our dark brown hair
retreating to the small trees
for reprieve
we snack on smoked salmon
berries
something I found at the
local all organic store
they are one of my greatest love stories
it is years full of
tears
laughter
babies
grief
ceremony
dancing
talking
being

Oh, Kay

deadleh nehiyawi accent
full of compassion
forgiveness
humour
love

enough for a whole community
to heal

S/He

Was born
On spring equinox
This doesn't surprise me
The languid dancer
Between worlds
The bringer of Spring's sunlight
While embracing
Winter's long, cold darkness
The giver of love
Joy
Art
Meaning
My beautiful Beric
Birthed
On the most perfect date
Look at all of us
Two-legged ones
Four-legged ones
Feathered ones
Mother Earth
Celebrating you
Every year

J

Was never good with words
He mostly enjoyed
Chasing
Devouring
Me
In the woods
The backseat
The stairway
Wherever he could
Cause I tasted like nothing
He ever had in his 32 years
But once
He said, when he was not mine,
When you came out of that lodge
Your skin flushed from the steam
Your hair like a crown
Set up against the sun
Your yellow dress
Clinging to your curves
I fell in love with you, again
And remembered why
Men started wars
over women
Who look like you

Year 1 without Sharron.

She Let Us Make Stars.

It's been nearly a year.
What does that look like to you? That time.
A walk in the meadow?
Is sunlight streaming on your peach sun-kissed face?
Arms sprawled out, fingertips grazing overgrown wheat in a
Wildflower patch. A confused scenery. The way it was meant
to be.
Did it feel like a heartbeat? The first strike on a drum?
A minuscule pause in time?
Half a breath?
With your smile, full, just as it was—still is, was how you
looked in this dream.
Carefree. Beautiful.
The year here, for us, was not as easy.
But I do not want you to worry.
Listen to our prayers. Guide us. Love us.
Just as you always have.
Now when we say, "the ancestors hear you."
It's you.
You are the ancestors.

THE SECOND ROUND

GIVING GRATITUDE

**Motherhood, My children, Myself
and the Many Forms of Love**

Beyond Existence

My life
is
curated
to the
ways
I want
mountains
tea
community
blind folded yoga
my children
Time and energy
are precious gifts
I only give
To whom I choose

Should

suffocates
the way I should
mother
leaves me
deciding
drive/cash/drive/crash
should
lands me hospitals
should
stifles
with its rigid ways
born 4 weeks and 4 days
late
I never was one
who does what she should
I do what I want
when I so please

Moon Children

I wonder if moon children know
How close they follow the tide of their mother
They are her favourite sights and sounds
Andromeda
The pipes, both small and large
Saturn with its ring
Even cold Mars with its red magik
Her gifts
Eternal

Scars

She wears her
Mother's scars
Wanting to die
Since she was seven years old
Or fall asleep
Letting go of the time passed by
Until the hurt
Sense of perceived
Abandoning
Dissipates
Thinking she could love them
Enough for herself
Themselves
And him
It was not
Not even close enough
And now her daughter wears
Her mother's scars

Break Ups

I cut her strawberries
in the hopes
Mohawk Medicine
can do something
for her bruised
heart

Pierce

So quiet
so sweet
I worry you get left behind
lost
in silence
driven to get
everyone to notice how
amazing you are

London

My little, blue eyed iskwew
Freckles and blonde hair
The manifestation of my
Swedish blood
With Ceremonial songs
Both Tradish and Machine made
Ingrained in her
by nine years old
Throws on Fleetwood Mac
"Mom, let's just cruise west"
My little highway girl

Daughters

I want my daughters
to have the attitude
of punk rock
and the grace
to carry it
like a sunflower
reaching for the sun

Lilacs

I typically thrive in fields of
raven roses and orchids
But
There is something
about the pink and purple lilacs
who were caught in a cross wind
as I birthed my fourth blessing
at home surrounded by
women who loved him, me
Every year I am reminded
of my own strength
caught on the cross wind

Webs and Fire Starters

Motherhood has been a series of
Cracked windshield
 Destructive webs
Allow fractured thoughts
                              Lights
                    Memories
Seep through more blurred lines of tears
                    Rage
          Fear
Uncertainty
Then of bliss and dreamy archetypes

I soak myself in hot water
Saturated in calendula, sea salt and oils
To repair matches striking my skin
Fiery fists aim for my face as the ever present
I hate you
I wish you were dead
land, searing my ears

Phoenix

for a week I slathered
you in bear grease and
eucalyptus oil.
smudge heavy in the
air.
snuggles and naps.
I wish I could heal you
from all this anger
in the same way.
but, I cannot
and I am so sorry

Chael

when your baby looks like your father
you want to heal his hurts
to take away the memories
of a mother who abandoned
a father's hands who beat
kids who tormented and called names
By being a gentle, caring mother
one whose hands are steady

full of love
maybe it will heal all the hurts
of a father
of my childhood
he never meant to be

Play

mud squished toes
river washed hands
laughter in abundance
sunsets painted by Sky Mother
warm campfires
sleepy papoose
me, smiling
healing

Who Are You?

I'm a poetic, esoteric, spiritual
star-being that has an arduous time
not returning to the skies. I stand on the
top of mountains to reach and touch
the nearest nebula in order to stop myself
from leaving entirely. As a child I
believed I controlled the wind and would
test the loyalty of the gods and goddesses
by demanding weather changes while I lay in
the grass, interpreting the secret
messages in the clouds
convinced I was left behind by accident.

THE THIRD ROUND

THE HOT ROUND

Relationships: Fantasy, Dating, Sex, Break Ups
and Picking up the Pieces

Metaphysical

I grew up atheist
Which comes as a surprise
My introduction to something
More than me was Ouija boards
Cold creatures pulling my leg under
Tarot cards read on top of the pentagram
Spirits looking for their lost child
Bright lights in the night skies
So
Don't be surprised when I don't want
To be lit like sage
Tumbling smoke
Held gently
And
I want to be Lillith
Powerful
On top
In control
Of my own
Pleasure
Where
You
Only
Wish
To
Be

A Chance

I want you
More than pings
And hearts
I wanted a first
awkward date
concerts
hikes
late night baths
reading you poetry
I just wanted you
That's all

Healer

Gently, they took their thumb
Ran it up and over every knuckle
My palm opens
Pressed their lips in the centre
Now, let's see what we can do
To heal you

Give me that gnarly man

Nice
Doesn't
Like poetry
About spanking
Gnarly
Replies,
"That pink mark."

Tinder & Tacos

In the time of
Tinder and tacos
can I get some
love and loyalty?

Good Morning

I adore
   crave
     want
    idolize
  love
    relish
      yearn
        covet
     desire
   hunger
pine
  savour
    appreciate
        enjoy
        morning sex

Witchy Women

These Witchy women

with Raven hair

    Sunlit hair

      Scarlet hair

    Messy and unbound

Have particular needs

Candles

Binding leather

Deep red lips

Under the protection of the moonlight

Witnessed at every phrase

To feel their love unleashed

While tied

Is a Ceremony

Few are fortunate to receive an invite for

Worship

You worship at her feet

You worship her feet

You worship her

Worship her

Worship

her

Women as Mountains

Mountains
Are women
Laying naked
On their back
Side
Lush green bushes
Wet blue lakes
White nipple peaks
Dark caves
Sacred
Explorations

Awoken

she kissed her back
tracing her
fingertip
from shoulder
tip
to
shoulder tip
she could hear the
slight shift in her
breath
from gentle
rhythmic
to shallow
anticipation
where those
lips
and fingertips
would next explore

Trickster

He wasn't a bad spirit, after all.
But still a trickster.
Shape shifting his way into her bed
And her head.

Puzzled Piece

When you told her

You are my missing puzzle piece

Where sky meets ground

   My horizon

     My Moon

     My Star

What happens when she walks away?

Back to the supernova she was conceived in that

Has the most beautiful moonsets

She's still whole

Sweet smile, lovely morning messages, maddening gorgeous

What happens to you?

You look for her in sunsets, sunrises, poetry

     Failing

   Miserable

Right back where she found you

Act Right

I laid my
Heart
Fears
Tobacco
Down
For you

You acted as though you've never seen ceremony before

One Day

One day I won't be here
In pieces strewn
Across the floor
Scrambling to pick them up
Morsels bonded by grief, shame and the unwavering belief,
he never would
Fragments visible by the glint they make in the sunlight
Cradled in my palm
Bloodied, frayed fingers
Always fixing, always repairing
Wiping tears
For all those years

Scar Upon Scar

I peeled back my flesh
broke my own bone
removed the marrow that
held onto you

and began again

Exhale

I'd wake to you
Lying on your stomach
Half covered in sheets
Gently tracing my chin
Following my jawline upwards
Caressing my earlobe
Up and over the tops of my ears
Slowly sweeping my cheekbone

I'd look at you through half-open eyes
Not wondering what you were doing

Because your eyes
Show the disbelief
Of me here in your bed
Still
After all these years
Of what ifs, bad timing, could haves
I'm now here
And very much real

No more restless nights
4am wake ups
Lonely

The quiet
Is broken
By your exhaled
"I love you"

Sex is Ceremony

Sex is powerful
Sex is healing
Sex is fun
Sex is love
Sex is intimate
Sex is giving
Sex is receiving
Sex is sacred
Sex is Ceremony

THE FOURTH ROUND

SEND THE ANCESTORS HOME

The Ceremony that Held Me Through it All

Writing Process

burn your medicines
let your truth spill

Surrender

there is no door
to call open
there is no breaking
a fast
there is no call
to support and switch
there is, you
baby
and the
ceremony
that is
birth

The lies we feed fear

as you find the
edge of discomfort
explore
breathe
release
and then
lean into it
just a little bit more
let it shift
into a place
of
comfort

Year 2 without Sharron, Mama Two Shoes.

The sunrise was her gift to the grieving.

This morning, as we lit sage, cedar and sweetgrass
all picked, braided and ground by my hand
we gave our prayers to you
you always showed us
how warm, beautiful and bold your love truly is

Grandfather Stones

My soul is safe
nurtured for
By the grandfather stones
Whose spirits I lay on my chest
To keep me from ascending
Into the night sky

Grandmother Moon

she greets me
in her light
gives the space
to rest
release
everything
and reminds me
I am whole
in every
phase

Webs

Grandmother spider,
I wish I had never-ending
Creativity
Your endless supply of
Silky string
Is jealousy provoking
I watch,
You, without effort,
Nimbly
Lay out a pattern, that's never
To be duplicated
Your delicate, intricate, sinewy web
Is a force of nature
And if done by sunrise
Its place to catch the morning dew
A shimmering sight to behold
I only wish to create something similar
To catch
The occasional haiku

Look, even when we aren't asking for medicine, we receive them

I had a dream that I was eating soup infused with sweet grass, a whole braid. I was explaining, softly, to a little brother, seated beside me, why there were medicines in my soup. He looked at his soup, took his spoon in his chubby little hand and proceeded to scoop out a delicate, warm, soft piece of meat. This sweet little one smiled in delight, recognizing the gift.

Reciprocity

Bring me the trees.
Their roots underfoot, stronger than the
winds sent from the Ocean, providing
strength for over 800 years.
Upon my death
Let my body rot in the trees; so I
may return to the mother,
nourishing the dirt, releasing my soul to
dance back to the ancestors.
The natural balance of life and death
Continues

ABOUT THE AUTHOR

Alycia Two Bears is a member of Mistawasis Nêhiyawak First Nation but calls Mohkinstsis home. She identifies as a mixed-blooded iskwew; her mother, Karen Hines, is a white settler of Swedish descent, and her father is Keith Head.

Alycia has a background in Education, completing her Bachelor of General Studies and Bachelor of Education at the University of Calgary.

As a Traditional apprenticing midwife and Clan Mother at The Moss Bag Project as Director of Traditional Health Wellness, every week Alycia and friends/kin/community create Moon Time Bags. These care packages for bleeding bodies who are houseless kin are handed out by grassroot community patrols. This is to support kin who may not have immediate access to menstrual health products and prevent theft charges to meet their basic body needs. Dignity and care of the community have brought together allies and community to support fundraising efforts and receive resources to make care packages that support bleeding bodies; pads, liners, tampons, underwear, chocolate, chapstick and sage smudge are the basics in these bags.

Raised in the late Sharron Proulx-Turners Sweat lodge, the teachings received in a Two Spirit, female-centred and run are near and dear to her heart; The safest place to grow spiritually, particularly as a bisexual, Indigiqueer Two Spirit.

As a Poet, she has earned an Honorable Mention in the 2020 Kemosa Scholarship for Indigenous Mothers in Alberta. Alycia was a contributor to the Matriarchy Edition of Winnipeg's Red Rizing Magazine. This connection led to Alycia leading an online night of self-care and poetry for femmes and females on Valentine's Day in 2022.

A regular contributor to New Tribe Magazine she has written articles about colonization, MMIW2S, Two Spirit history, terms and community support that accompanies these topics. Her poetry included in New Tribe has been driven by the love of her community. Her latest poetry piece was published in Marigolde's collection, *Wilding and Sprout: Pregnancy loss, Abortion and Postpartum Poetry Anthology,* a community created fundraiser with 100% of proceeds being donated to organizations dedicated to reproductive justice and expanding access to abortion care for BIPOC and LGBTQIA+ individuals.

9 781738 858712